Your First
90 Days
In Your New Job

(This is the shortest book you will
ever need to get there)

I dedicate this book to all the managers
who have worked for me. I appreciate
and respect the work that you have
done. I do know that all of you will
continue to demonstrate the success you
have known during our partnership. I
would also like to mention the great
companies that I have worked for and
have helped me prove my management
style.

Amazon.com
GATX
Brightpoint
Target
Pamida
Office Depot

This is a short book. It is meant to be a short book. You don't need a lot of fluff. You will hear enough of that daily from your managers and the people who work for you and with you.

It is not the size it is the lesson. Take something away from this book, use it and modify it to make it work for you. When you have found a solution for you, then try and teach someone else so they can develop a style.

Just as the world is round, when you do something positive for someone, something positive will come back to you.

The same goes the other way as well. When you do something to undermine someone or cause him or her some injustice, that too will come back to you.

What you won't find in this book:

- You won't find a lot of charts and graphs whose meaning you struggle to understand.
- You won't find a lot of words that don't really mean anything but are there to make the book look bigger.
- You won't find a lot of psychiatric theory that goes against your own experience, making you feel like you are not aware of what is going on around you.
- You won't find all the answers to all your questions.

You will find in this book:

- A way to start your first 90 days on your new job.
- A way, based on experience of how you can deal with certain situations you will come up against during your new position.

You passed the interview, got the job, now it is time to earn your pay!

DAY 1

Day 1 is a meet and greet day. You will be introduced to your peers and your new team.

There are responsibilities on Day 1 for both you and your employer.

Day 1 - **Company Responsibilities**:

1. Provide you with benefits paperwork to review and sign.

2. Provide you with your working space. (Some companies, depending on your management level, may have your desk area on the production floor, or you may have an office or cubical assigned to you).

3. Provide you with an access badge, security codes (if needed), keys to the building (if needed), a laptop or personal computer, systems access codes and finally, email access.

4. Depending on your management level, you may be assigned an administrative assistant. If so,

make it a point to spend some time with that person on day one, as they will become critical to your success.

Day 1 - **Your Responsibilities**

On Day 1 you have responsibilities as well. Observation will be one of the major things you will do. It will play a key role in your success.

Your other responsibilities are:

1. **Assess the situation**. When you interviewed, you were not given all the gory details of the state of the facility. On day 1 you have the chance to see things as they really are.

2. **Go to your department and observe, watch the people who will be working for you.** Introduce yourself and ask questions about what they are doing (it doesn't matter whom you ask, just ask). Be sure to ask what they like and don't like about their jobs because now that is your burden to bear.

3. **Start sizing up your peers** (the ones on your level). Be aware of the way they dress, the way they speak, how they carry themselves. Using your strengths, assess where you see your fit. Remember, it is only day 1 and most people will be on their best behavior because they are sizing you up as well.

The following are Objectives for Day 1:

1. Take care of your benefits paperwork.
2. Get your systems access.
3. Take a walk around the facility.
4. Observe your department in action.
5. Make notes of your observations.
6. Start getting settled into your workspace.
7. Evaluate your peer competition.

Day 2 – Day 5

Day 2 - Day 5 will consist mostly of your meeting with your team and establishing yourself as the new leader.

The first two weeks are the most critical for a new manager. Your team expects you to come in and make some changes. This is also the timeframe when they determine what your management style is.

If you don't take advantage of your opportunity during the first two weeks then you will have to fight an uphill battle to gain the respect and control of your department. Keep in mind; your new team knows nothing about you. They will assume that you are the best candidate the company could find.

You also have to keep in mind that there are other people who interviewed for your position and didn't get the job. Those people want to see why they were passed over; unfortunately, it is your job to demonstrate to them that they are not yet ready for your position.

You have some decisions to make:

1. **What management style will you use**? Will you come in and be a dictator? Will you come in and be laid back? Will you have to develop some new tools for your management style?

2. **What goals are you trying to achieve**? Will you have to drive productivity in all areas or a few areas? Do you have to improve morale? Is cost something you have to tackle?

3. **What timeframe are you considering to achieve your goals?** Were you hired in a crisis situation? If so, you may not have 90 days and you will most assuredly have to have a plan. Do you have longer than 90 days to get to where you need to be? What is your timeframe?

4. **How will you communicate to your new team?** Will you have a meeting on day one and introduce yourself? If so, what do you say in that meeting? Do you wait a few days and allow yourself to be introduced by your manager? If the

option is open, I recommend that you introduce yourself to the team on your own. People like to see that you are going to make decisions and be involved.

During Days 2 – 5 you also need to get updates on your staffing. You will want to find out about reviews, pay rate changes and disciplinary actions as well as attendance issues.

The following are Objectives for Day 2 – Day 5:

1. **Get the current status of your team**. You will want to know if any of your associates are on the bubble of being terminated. You will also need to know the facts of their disciplinary actions. It is important to be aware of the reasons because some associates have a tendency to repeat bad behavior. If you know what that behavior is ahead of time, you can immediately apply the appropriate discipline.

2. **Check to see if all your team reviews are up to date**. Associates tend to get upset when they are due a bonus, raise or an

evaluation and they don't get one on time.

3. **Get data to see how your team has been performing over the last two months.** This will give you a starting point to quantify your impact and should include Safety, Quality and Productivity data.

4. **Get an understanding of the attendance policy and disciplinary process**. Set up a meeting with Human Resources if there is no handbook available.

5. **Start establishing goals based on your data findings and the facility goals.** Goals are important. If you walk in the door with a plan and some goals that you can communicate to your team you are earning points.

Now that your first week is over, you will want to set the tone for the first 30 days. In order to be a successful manager, you should understand what drives your department.

For example, if your department's success depends upon another department's performance, you want to fully understand the scope of that impact. You want to know that because when your department does not perform well (and it sometimes may not) you want to be able to explain "the miss" (*any negative variation to your goal*) in detail.

Far too many managers can't explain with sufficient detail why the miss occurs. Usually a manager, who is not as engaged as he/she should be, will find a reason to blame it on something outside their control. When you are the boss, however, all things fall under your control. If you want to be a manager that is seen as knowledgeable about his/her department, then you will want to explain your miss in a more detailed manner.
Example of a Basic Response to a Miss:

Let's say your team was supposed to ship 30,000 cartons but they only shipped 27,000 and your manager asks you, "What happened?"

A basic answer would go like this, "We had a lot of people call out yesterday and the new people we have don't work as fast as everyone else".

This statement prompts many questions such as:

1. How many people called out?

2. What was the actual rate of productivity for yesterday and what impact did the new people have?

3. Do we have training issues?

4. Did we communicate earlier In the shift that we had a staffing shortage?

5. What part of production was affected most?

6. Could we have shifted people?

7. Did we use overtime?

Example of a Detailed Response to a Miss:

Let's say your team was supposed to ship 30,000 cartons but they only shipped 27,000 and your manager asks you, "What happened?"

We had 4 people call out and, at an expected 675 cartons per person per day, this accounts for 2700 of the 3000 carton miss. We also have 3 new people who only processed at 47 cartons per hour out of an 84 carton per hour productivity rate. This accounts for the remaining 300 cartons. There will be follow up training and feedback for the 3 new associates.

We did check with other departments for resources but all departments were tapped. We chose not to use OT because it was too late to have the associates adjust their schedules.

See how the answer above is much more detailed and does not prompt as many questions. This is how you want to explain details of your department. It will make your manager much more confident in your abilities to manage your team.

Day 6 – Day 10

The following are Objectives for Day 6 – Day 10:

1. **Learn your managers' idiosyncrasies** (likes, dislikes, pet peeves).
   a. Figure out what kind of management style they are trying to use with you.
   b. Ask your manager what level of detail they expect from you.
   c. Ask them how they define success.

2. **Get familiar with the reports that your manager uses to base your performance.**

3. **Check with other managers to see what they are using to track their performance.** This can work to your advantage in several ways.
   a. You don't have to recreate the wheel.
   b. You gain knowledge about the competition.
   c. You will get a chance to weed out the team players from the non-team players. The team players will share their spreadsheets and tracking information. The non-team players will try to explain how to do it and have you go through the process by starting from scratch.

Your First 15 Days

In your first 15 days, one of the key things that will earn you the respect of your team is for you to go out to their departments and work beside them. This has several benefits.

1. You will gain a better understanding of what your associates do.
2. You will be feeling their "pain" and be more able to respond to it.

3. It will give you credibility when you change a process.

You will want to work in each department. You are responsible for a minimum of 4 hours in each department. Ask a lot of questions, let your team see that you are human but don't get "chummy".

You want your teams to respect you; you don't want to be their pal. You don't want to be their enemy either but, in order for you to lead effectively, you need to establish yourself as the head of the team and initially that requires some distance.

Day 11 – Day 15

The following are objectives for you to meet during days 11-15:

1. **Establish the initial relationship with your team.**
    - Have a meeting with your entire team.
    - Tell them about yourself. (Your experience, maybe your family).
    - Expect some criticism (most associates usually are not very trusting or open to a new manager).

- Be very up front and honest; don't try to make things seem better than they are. Associates can read through BS better than anyone.

Things to expect during that first meeting with your team:
- Expect some comments or questions you may feel are inappropriate for an initial meeting. Your new team will expect you to know some things that you have no way of knowing. For these questions simply respond, "I don't know but will find out and provide you with an answer as soon as I have one".
- Expect your new team to not believe a thing you are saying.
- Remember some of your associates probably had a manager that they were very fond of or disliked. Most people don't like change so you may get resistance. Don't let this bother you; they know you are in charge. But also remember, you are establishing yourself with this team and if they see

weakness then they will eat you alive.

2. **Learn the processes for each department using the "hands on" method.**
   - If you are already able to determine who will be your most challenging associates (*associates that are not very open to your being on the team*), have them show you the process that they work in. They will try and show you up and that is okay; in fact, initially it is to your benefit to be shown up. The reason you are choosing your most difficult associate is because they usually have influence over a majority of the group and when you show them you are ready to make things better, then others will support your efforts.

3. **Start to track the metrics of your department.** (Data is a very effective tool for review time.)

Days 16 – 30

During this time period you will be observing, assessing and data gathering. To help you, you have to first assess your own strengths and weaknesses. The reason you have to assess yourself is because you want to make an honest comparison when sizing yourself up against your peers.

Questions you should ask yourself:

1. **What are my strengths?** Your real ones, the ones that no matter what will come through for you.
2. **What weaknesses do I have?** Okay this is a hard one; most of us don't like to admit we have any weaknesses, so why don't we call them "areas of opportunity" from now on?
3. **What skills do I have?** For example, if you know how to build spreadsheets or you are good with PowerPoint, these are skills. You don't have to be the best at them, but you would certainly be ahead of anyone who has no skill in these areas.

4. **Do I have a plan?**

Now that we have some of the questions let's look at them in more detail.

1. **What are your strengths?** Your real strengths, the strengths that no matter what will come through for you. What Skills do you possess?

Every manager has a skill that they are good at. The problem is that there is usually only one and it is not developed as time goes by. Think about a time in your career, no matter how long or short, when you felt that you accomplished something that was in your eyes fantastic, awesome or a career milestone.

Do you have the ability to make quick decisions? This is what good managers do all the time. I am not saying that all managers, even good ones, don't make the occasional bad decision but the key to their success is that they make quick decisions, which are usually good ones.

Some managers are numbers driven and are good at it but have terrible people skills. Some managers are fantastic at people skills but terrible with numbers and metrics. Some managers are good at motivating people and building teams but not able to discipline. Some managers are really good "go getters", fast movers but are so worried about their own success they don't try and develop their managers or associates for the "next" level. (Don't be this manager.)

2.   **What weaknesses do you have?**

Okay this is a hard one; most of us don't like to admit we have any weaknesses, so why don't we call them "areas of opportunity" from now on? ☺

No one knows you better than you! As managers, we sometimes don't admit to our shortcomings for one reason or another.

Well the times, they are a-changing. He who asks for help gets it, and the squeaky wheel does get the grease. If you ask for help it can work in your favor. Whether you are in front of your peers or in front of your boss, do not be afraid to ask for assistance or ask questions. It shows that you are willing to ask for assistance rather than make a decision that you are not certain is correct.   Don't suffer in silence.

What about your computer skills? Are you strong in Word, Excel and PowerPoint? I didn't ask are you familiar with it? I asked are you strong in it. Listening is a skill everyone needs to master.

If you don't listen you can miss out on valuable information as well as opportunities to shine. If you are trying to progress in a company you have to listen and observe

3. Do I have a plan?

Plan, Plan, Plan – Planning is key to your success. You should plan everything you can: plan for success, plan for failure, have back up plans, plan ahead, plan what you are going to say before you say it, plan for responses to questions, plan for surprises.

If you have a plan, you can be successful because it is according to your PLAN!!!!!

Other things to look out for during days 16 – 30:

Don't assume everything that is told to you is accurate or true. Find out for yourself, verify things that sound a little incorrect.

> – Question things you don't understand, even if you think that it is a stupid question (within reason). Ask because you will have the answer and other people in the room will be drawn to you as a person who doesn't let their pride

stand in the way. Even if everyone else in the room knows the answer, but you are not sure, ask the question because then <u>you</u> will know.

– Challenge someone's findings if they differ from your own. This will give you an opportunity to learn something that you don't know. Don't allow someone to tell you that their information is the best information when your data shows different conclusions.

If asked a question to which you don't know the answer, don't make something up, say you don't know.

- Your responsibility when you say you don't know is to find out. The next time you will know. You never want to get caught off guard on the same issue.

- If you do know the answer, then state it briefly and with as much detail as you can.

- If you are in a room with others and a manager who has been with the company starts to answer, yield to that person. It does not make you subservient;

it is out of courtesy. If you try to
answer every question, it makes
you seem like a smart ass; if you
answer no questions at all, it
makes you look subordinate to
your peers. Mix it up and be
active in the conversation as
much as you can.

Don't get too friendly with any of your
peers during the first 30 days.

- I didn't say don't make friends. I
  said don't get too friendly.
  Remember, during this
  timeframe you are still sizing up
  your peers and they, believe it or
  not, are sizing you up as well.
  Go on the occasional lunch but
  don't go out after work unless it
  is a group outing. Remember,
  perception is truth to some
  people. If your peers see that
  you want to go to the bar after
  work everyday it could be
  perceived that you have a
  drinking problem (weakness). If
  you don't go out on occasion
  then you could possibly be
  perceived as stuck up or make
  people think you are too good to
  hang out with them
  (individualistic).
  Don't go out after work if you

really don't want to. Never do something that you absolutely don't want to do and don't lie about it. If you don't want to hang out because you want to be with your family, then simply say you want to spend time with your family.

Now that you have done so much to get to day 31 let me first say congratulations! ☺

Trust me, your hard work will pay off. You should be seeing the following results from all your efforts if you applied the strategies outlined for Day 1 – Day 30:

- You know who your problem children are on your team and you should have a plan (at least in your head) as to how you are going to deal with them.

- The rest of your team is providing ideas for improvements without your initializing the conversation.

- You have a way to track your data daily.

- You have an established milestone (or your starting point).

- You have set goals that you have communicated to your team.

- You have good knowledge of the processes that you manage.

- You have an idea of areas that can be improved.

- You have an initial assessment of the strong and weak managers that are your competition.

You should complete all these checkpoints before moving on to the next phase.

Day 31 – Day 60

You are now at a point where you feel more comfortable in your new facility. You should be comfortable around your boss and your peers.

Start Day 31 with vigor. Your goal during this time frame is to start leading your team to improvement.

How should you do it? Do you have a plan?

Okay, you bought this book so I could help you, so here is what I suggest.

- Take the data that you've been tracking in your first 30 days and compare it to the goals you should have received from your manager. For all the data that is under goal, those are priority opportunities for you. For all the data that is above goal, those are also opportunities but they are not priorities at this time.
  o With the "priority" data, determine which one has the biggest negative impact to Safety, Quality or Productivity. (*Hint: This is where all the detailed information and understanding of your department comes in*) Now that you know which area is affecting your department the most, you can focus on that or create a focus group of associates to help you identify causes and possible solutions.
- Have a meeting with your team and explain where the impacted areas are. Explain what fixing those areas will do overall for the department and have some type of reward for them should they reach the goal you set. (*Hint:*

Pizza only works a few times; most associates like things with the company name on them: pens, T-shirts, coffee mugs etc.)

- Use the information as a motivation tool. If your team is working large amounts of overtime, you can explain how overtime will reduce when you have achieved your goal. Associates want to see light at the end of the tunnel.

If your team has been giving you feedback (positive and negative), you should have that feedback documented and roll out your plan for addressing the issues.   You can do that in the following ways:

- You can announce in meetings what associate recommended suggestions are being worked on.
- You can post the ideas on a board for everyone to see.
- You can announce at start up meetings or your end of week meetings.
- You can provide gift certificates to the associates that submitted their ideas.

Start small achievable group projects. An example of a small group project would be having a few of your team focus on the morale or set the rewards for achieving various levels of success. It doesn't really matter what. Get your teams started now!

Right around days 45-50, you will want to look at the progress of your departments. You set the data starting point earlier. Now you should see what improvements have been made.

Example is: If your data showed that your team was processing orders at 70 orders per hour and now you are processing 80 orders per hour, that is a 10 order per hour improvement or a 14.2% improvement over where you started. You should be able to answer some questions now. How did you get this improvement? If you did several things, how did each thing that you did contribute to your overall improvement?

For Example: If one of the things you did was to change shift hours, then what impact did that have? If you changed a process, how did that process change reflect in your improvement numbers? Remember to document the things you do and document the progress or regress that happen. Things just don't get better.

Be able to explain in detail where the impact is.

During this period you should have been able to determine the management style of your manager. This is important because it will be an aid in determining how fast you will move up (or out) in a company. Here are a few manager types to look out for:

1. **The Laid Back Manager** – This is the manager who lets you make all the decisions and says, "Keep me informed". They say that because when their manager asks them what is going on they can give a decent answer. This is a good manager to work for if you have a good handle on your people and a good feel for the pulse of your facility. It is good because you will have his job if you can allow yourself a little time. Managers like this are just biding time. They don't want to be promoted; they are comfortable with where they are and what they are getting paid. As companies move forward, this type of manager will become obsolete. If you want to be highly successful with this manager

then play into his weakness. Run your department the way you choose to run it, as long as it is successful and within company policy. Make all the changes that you want because this type of manager won't even notice.

2. **The Ready, Fire, Aim Manager** – This is the type of manager that makes decisions without facts. They think they know everything and will make decisions based on nothing except what they believe to be correct, no matter what you tell them. You have to be careful around this manager because they don't like to be wrong, don't like to put other people's ideas into action and feel that you are very expendable. If you have this type of manager, what you can do is give them the information that they ask for when they ask for it, and document anything that you don't agree with but are directed to do.

3. **The Popular Manager** – This manager is a good manager to work for. The associates like

them, the managers like them, they make decisions and, even when those decisions come out badly, their people support them. This type of manager is someone to model some of your future management style after. There is a downside though; sometimes this manager, in his/her quest to please those that work for them, will sometimes make the popular decision instead of the right decision. If you happen to work with this type of manager congratulations, you will have a good opportunity to see how to do things the right way. Just take care of your department and your people.

4. **The Hard Nose Manager** – This manager seems like they have a chip on their shoulder. They are very direct and seem mean on the outside. They are usually very knowledgeable and come with a lot of respect. If you have this type of manager, coming to work may seem harder but you will learn more because they are demanding and will want you to do things the right way. When you have worked for this type of

manager for a year or so, you
will see that when you are in the
next level position that you find
yourself being more detailed and
your style of management will
change.

There is no best type of manager for
all people; it depends on how you
are and where your weaknesses are.

Days 61 – 90

Okay you are in the homestretch now. ☺ I am proud of you.   During this period all things come to a point.

- You have sized up your fellow managers.

- You have sized up your associates.

- You have determined the management style of your manager.

- You have started tracking your success.

- You are communicating with your team daily.

- You are providing feedback daily.

- You have established your career plan.

- You are tracking your projects.

You are at a point where you should be, which is standing out among your peers.

Your manager should be noticing this and giving you more responsibility. This may not sound like something positive but with responsibility comes authority and with authority comes power. Power is what you want.

DEALING WITH THE BACKSTABBERS

Every company has backstabbers. They are the people that are always smiling at you and talking to you, then at first opportunity they turn on you. A good example goes something like this.

Let's say you have a project that you are working on and the due date is 2 days away. You realize that you won't make the deadline, go to one of your peers for help and he/she says they will help you. They talk about all the different things they can do to help you make the deadline. Time goes by and the help they promised never comes. They go to your boss and tell them that your part of the project won't be finished and it will impact the whole project. When approached by your manager, you explain that you asked for help but the other person has already placed a negative thought in the manager's head. Now a good manager will listen to your side of the story and not let what anyone says to them make a difference. A poor manager will take what anyone tells them and start making assumptions without fact.   The most important thing about dealing with back stabbers is "keep your friends close and your enemies closer". I have personally found that if you directly confront the backstabber, they have a tendency to not backstab you again. Backstabbers will have less opportunity to screw you over if you are taking care of your responsibilities.

SETTING PRIORITIES

There is nothing difficult about setting priorities. I have read books where there is a big deal about how to do it and formulas for getting the best results on priority setting. Please.

The process for setting priorities is simple. **"The person who has most control over your progression in the company is your priority".** Look at it like this, if you fall behind on a project for one of your peers, you don't get in trouble, they do. All they can do is point the finger back at you but the ultimate responsibility is theirs to deliver. Now on the other hand, if you drop a project for your boss and he gets the royal butt chewing from his boss, you can most likely say good-bye to that promotion you were up for. See how that works?

DEALING WITH THE BROWN NOSERS

People who brown nose can be a source of entertainment; they can also cause you more work than you need. I should state that there is a difference between a brown noser and a person that needs attention. The brown noser says and does things that make his/her boss feel good. They don't always have the facts and will always make themselves look good as long as the boss needs that. The attention getter is someone who is insecure about his or her skills or their placement in the organization. They usually do good work but want to make sure that someone notices. Once they get the attention or recognition from their boss they are pretty content. You can deal with the brown noser by letting them do what they are going to do and enjoy it until it starts affecting you, then you must go to the brown noser and let them know how their weakness is impacting your life. The result will be that they are less likely to do things that impact you.

DEALING WITH THE LESS PRODUCTIVE

Someone on your team is bound to be the weakest link. When you have a weak link you need to address it immediately or it will spread like poison. There are different ways to address improvements; you don't want to single the person(s) out if you don't have to, but there will be times when you do have to single them out. When that time comes, you will want to remain professional but let them know that they are impacting the rest of the team. At that point peer pressure will play a part. Make sure that you are providing them with all the support and training they need to be successful.

TAKE RISKS

Many managers make the mistake of not trying new things for fear of getting into trouble. I have never seen a person get terminated for trying something new to improve the morale, safety, productivity or quality. Think outside of the box. Try something; many of your managers will appreciate you trying something that will advance the department. DO NOT let yourself fall into the trap of doing it the same way because everyone else did. Check with your manager to see how much flexibility you have to make your department better. Work with other managers so you can get their buy in.

You are going to run into situations where you have to deal with some issues that are going to impact another person. You are going to have to have hard conversations with peers, managers and your subordinates.

I have a good amount of experience delivering the hard message. It never gets easier.

One of the hardest conversations to have with a person is about their personal hygiene. It sounds like an easy conversation but it will truly be the hardest conversation you will have, especially when the person is of the opposite sex.

If you have to have a conversation like that, put one thought in your mind first. *If someone had to talk to you about your hygiene, how would you want him or her to tell you?*

It can't be easy for anyone to hear that they smell or they are unclean. When you have this conversation the other person can take it in a negative way. Don't pass the buck. Don't tell them someone else made you do it. The process should look something like this.

Step one: Call them into your office or a private place where no one else can hear. DO NOT answer your phone, pager or allow anyone to enter that private area. DO NOT check emails or have anything in your office or area that will distract you.

Step two: If the person is of the opposite sex, have peers of the opposite sex in the room with you. It is best to have someone from Human Resources in the office in case there are issues. It should be someone that most people like, if possible; it makes it easier on the recipient to receive the message.

Step three: Be prepared. This person already thinks that they are in trouble because you called them into the office. It only lengthens their insecurity and anxiety when you are not prepared.

Step four: Have an opening statement. Don't let it be a joke because it is not a joking matter.

Step five: Be direct and honest. Keep it short but not harsh. Keep in mind that this person has feelings and the way you deal with them today could build or break a bond between the two of you down the line. The conversation should go like this:

You: Good Morning, Jane.

Jane: Good morning.

You: Jane, I have been getting complaints from your peers and there are some things that I have noticed myself. I have to address them with you today.

Jane: What thing? Who is complaining? I'll bet it was Betty, wasn't it?

You: It doesn't matter who it was, that is not important. What is important is your personal hygiene. I have noticed that the last few days your clothing has had an offensive odor and your personal upkeep has not been the same. Is everything all right?

Jane: Are you telling me that I stink?

You: I am telling you that your body odor or the odor of your clothing has been offensive to your working environment.

Jane: So you are telling me I stink. Everybody on the floor or in the office does not smell like roses. Are you pulling

them in the office and telling them that
they stink too?

You: Jane, you are getting off the
subject. Let's deal with you and I right
now. We have to resolve this. Is
everything okay outside of work?

Jane: Look, I come to work everyday
and I work harder and faster than almost
everyone out there, so why pick me out
first?

You: Jane you are right, you are a very
good worker, and your attendance is
stellar. In fact, you have only missed one
day in two years. That is why it is very
hard for me to have this conversation. As
your manager I have to have it and it has
to be resolved today. I am not trying to
offend you; I am trying to inform you.

Jane: What do you want me to do?

You: I guess a better question to ask is
can we do anything for you, one of our
better employees?

Jane: Well, I work two jobs and I don't
have a lot of time to wash clothes when I
get home. Can you buy me a washer and
dryer so I can wash at home instead of at
the Laundromat?

You: No, we can't. I can refer you to our Employee Assistance Program and they may be able to assist you.

Jane: Okay.

You: Although I did not like the subject of our discussion, I am glad that we had a chance to talk. Next time let's make it about something positive, how's that?

Jane: That would be cool. So what do I do now?

You: I am going to let you go home and wash those clothes and take care of anything else you can today. Then I will see you bright and early in the morning.

Jane: Will I get paid?

Depending on what your company policy is, if any, it is your decision. Keep in mind if you make that decision for one, you make it for all. You could have the option of letting her make up the time during the week or pay her for leaving early due to the circumstances.

Step six: Follow up with Human Resources to see if Jane went to see them and follow up with Jane to see how things are going.

The subordinates who complained will come to you to see if you addressed the issue. You do not owe them a detailed explanation. You can simply say, "I handle all personal matters with privacy as I would do yours".

TERMINATING EMPLOYEES

When you have to terminate employees it can be a stress builder or a stress reliever. When it gets to the point where the associate needs to be terminated, the associate should know. It should come as no surprise to them that they are losing their job. If you as the manager or supervisor have been honest and upfront with your team and you have been fair, then you have nothing to worry about. If you have not been forthright and you want to terminate the associate because he/she made you look bad in front of your boss or team, that is wrong.

Regardless of what the associates say, they work because they need money or they need to be around people that they are comfortable with. When you remove someone from his or her job you should have a good, as well as documented, reason. This does not go for all cases. Some associates can do one thing that will cause them to get terminated. Fighting or blatant sexual harassment violations are just a few that will cause immediate termination.

When you have to terminate the associate, do it immediately. Don't wait until the end of the day (that truly pisses people off) and don't wait until lunch (however, if you do terminate around lunch time the associate will most likely not be missed until the next day). Be direct, be brief and have someone in the room with you, preferably someone from Human Resources.

The conversation should go something like this:

Step 1: Call the person into the office.

Step 2: Ask them to take a seat.

Step 3: Read directly from the termination letter (which has been approved by Human Resources). An example would be something like this:

On September 15, 2004 you were absent from work. On September 4, 2004 you were issued a final written warning stating that any further unexcused absence within 60 days would result in disciplinary action, up to or including termination.

As of today, September 15, 2004, your employment with A1B2C3 Company has been terminated.

Step 4: Collect any badges that they have to access the company or any keys. Escort the associate to the door and ensure that they leave the property. If you have a direct exit, use it. Do not walk the associate through the building; it gives the associate an opportunity to make a scene.

Step 5: Have all access to any systems terminated. Provide a termination letter to Human Resources.

Step 6: Contact security and let them know that the individual has been terminated and is not allowed on company property.

QUALITY TOOLS

There are other tools, which you should become familiar with: Six Sigma, Peoplesoft, and Kronos Time Management Systems.

SIX SIGMA – Six Sigma is defined as a statistical concept that measures a **process** in terms of **defects**. Six Sigma focuses on reducing and eliminating defects through practices that emphasize understanding, measuring, and improving processes.

Six Sigma has a core and it is based on the 5 phases of the projects that we will be completing. It is called the DMIAC process and it breaks down like this.
  D - Define
  M - Measure
  A – Analyze
  I – Improve
  C – Control

The DMAIC process takes away the mentality of "I think", "I feel", or "I believe", replacing it with quantifiable data.

My personal feeling about Six-Sigma is this: You don't need to be a Six Sigma Blackbelt or Greenbelt to be successful in your new role. It would help you to eliminate things in your department that are not providing you with the level of quality that you would like. You can read books on Root Cause Analysis, Six Sigma or you can track information over a period of time. If your performance is not where you want it to be and you can't figure out why, it is then time to run a project against it.

Okay, you have reached the end of this book. You should have some skills that will help you get noticed. Power is a wonderful thing and you get that via knowledge and good decision-making.

Good Luck with your career.

I would like to thank some of the managers who have worked for me. Thank you to:

James Werber – Amazon.com
Galen Hopkins – Amazon.com
Jeri Durren – Amazon.com

I will never forget the commitment to quality, safety and productivity you made with your teams, individually and collectively as a group. As you move on in your careers taking on facilities of your own, I can only hope that you will know the feeling I had when we did the impossible.

Justin Collier - Brightpoint
Jacque Bender – Brightpoint

Long nights with implementations, doing things from scratch. Your leadership proved essential. We would never have been able to achieve the things we did without your commitment.

Mark Raneo - GATX
Tim Goolesby – GATX

Who said that work couldn't be fun?? They never worked with us if they did. We were able to have fun and be successful in a very short period of time. Now you have your new success stories. I am very proud of you and glad to be a part of your development.

Rob Trautwein – PAMIDA

Rob, they said wc couldn't take the mess and fix it and we did; they said we couldn't get the 47 grand openings completed during the same time frame and we did it. Good leadership knows no bounds.

Eldridge Grady – Office Depot
James Smedley – Office Depot
Rodney Lovlie – Office Depot
Jaymar Moye – Office Depot
Don Goodwin – Office Depot
Mark Raneo – Office Depot
Tim Goolesby – Office Depot

Talk about a success story: a 90-day turnaround of morale, productivity, quality and safety. This happened because each manager was able to use his strengths enhanced by good supportive leadership. To go from 20th to 8th place in a 90-day timeframe was no small feat. We developed a culture and replaced an old one. Take the pride you felt when you saw the rise of our status and use it to develop your managers.

I would also like to thank some of the people who have influenced me to be a stronger manager and developer of managers.

Mark Howell,
President, Brightpoint Inc.

I always appreciated the fact that you spoke to your entire team as if you had known them forever. It always made me feel good about coming to work. It also made me feel good knowing that when I was leaving after an 18-hour day that you were leaving after an 18-hour day. I respect your interaction with people and your strong financial knowledge. Brightpoint allowed me to develop and grow in a growing company. Being a part of that growth has had a lasting impact on my career. Thank you.

John Sullivan,
Former EVP Operations, Brightpoint Inc.

I always respected the fact that you held everyone accountable. You were always direct. I thank you for supporting my promotions within the company. I was able to work and develop at the Director level. Thank you.

Jeff Wilke,
SVP Worldwide Operations, Amazon.com

The things I admire and respect about Jeff Wilke are far too many to mention here. I respect that he can, and sometimes will, be involved in projects that you are working on down to your level, no matter what that level is. He is no nonsense. When he says he is holding people accountable that means you, your manager, and his manager. Like most of senior management at Amazon, you can't give a basic answer. Detailed answers are expected. I also like that he has a presence. When he walks in a room all eyes are on him and when he speaks you can hear a pin drop. I don't think this is just due to his position in the company. I believe that it is the respect he has gained throughout his career. Due to his leadership, I hold my managers accountable on an entirely different level and I don't allow basic answers. Thank you.

Mark Mastandrea,
GM, Amazon.com UK

Because of Mark Mastandrea, I am a better people manager. Thanks to Mark, who is very knowledgeable, I was able to develop my diplomatic skills. I never thought that diplomacy was a key skill, but as your career moves upward and you are dealing with senior level executives, diplomacy is as important as knowledge. I have learned diplomacy, Mark, and you were right. Thank you.

Althea D'Souza,
Engineer, Amazon.com

I am lucky to know Althea D'Souza. She is one of the most intelligent people I know. Althea is able to take the most complicated processes, formulas, theory and everything else I can think of and break it down to the simplest form. Because of Althea I improved the way that I communicate with my managers and associates. Everyone learns differently and she was patient enough with me to make sure I learned that. Althea is also no nonsense. She expects things to be done on schedule. If you agree to a task, she has no mercy on you if you fail to complete it or ask for help in a untimely manner. I love that about her. Althea, I thank you for teaching me things that I will use forever. Thank you.

Bill Hutchinson,
CEO - ROBITRANZ INTERNATIONAL

If he were still alive, I would tell him that I have never met a man with so much drive. Bill was a hardnosed manager, very no nonsense. I don't think I ever appreciated the lessons I learned then as I do now. I only hope I am making you proud. Thank you for teaching without teaching.

Printed in the United States
126470LV00009B/247/A